Play It!

LEVEL 1

A Superfast Way to Learn
Awesome Songs on Your Guitar

CHRISTMAS SONGS

By Jennifer Kemmeter and Antimo Marrone

GRAPHIC ARTS BOOKS®

Turner Publishing Company
Nashville, Tennessee
www.turnerpublishing.com

Library of Congress Control Number: 2025011018

ISBN: 9781513141992 (paperback) | 9781513142005 (hardbound) | 9781513142012 (e-book)

Published by Graphic Arts Books
an imprint of West Margin Press

WEST
MARGIN
PRESS
WestMarginPress.com

jenniferkemmeter.com

0 1 2 3 4 5 6 7 8 9

Contents

INTRODUCTION TO THE GUITAR 6
   Tuning the Strings 7
   Color-Coding the Guitar 8
   Matching the TAB Staff to the Guitar Strings 9
PREPARING TO PLAY 10
PLAYING NOTES 12
NOTE TIMING AND NOTE LENGTH 13
   The Time Signature, Notes, and Measures 13
STRUMMING CHORDS 14
   Reading a Chord Chart 14
   Strumming Patterns and Time 15
SONGS WITH NOTES ON THE 3 LOWER STRINGS (G , B , E)
   1. *Up On the Housetop* 16
   2. *Good King Wenceslas* 18
   3. *Jolly Old Saint Nicholas* 20
   4. *We Three Kings of Orient Are* 22
   5. *Joy to the World* 24
   6. *Hark! The Herald Angels Sing* 26
   7. *O Come, All Ye Faithful* 28
   8. *The First Noel* 30
TOP TIPS FOR PLAYING NOTES 32
TOP TIPS FOR FRETTING 33
SONGS WITH NOTES ON THE 4 LOWER STRINGS (D , G , B , E)
   9. *Jingle Bells* 34
   10. *Auld Lang Syne* 36
   11. *It Came Upon a Midnight Clear* 38
   12. *O Christmas Tree* 40
   13. *Gloucestershire Wassail* 42
   14. *I Heard the Bells on Christmas Day* 44
   15. *I Saw Three Ships* 45
   16. *Deck the Halls* 46
   17. *Go Tell It on the Mountain* 48
   18. *Angels We Have Heard on High* 50
   19. *O Little Town of Bethlehem* 52
   20. *Ding Dong Merrily on High* 54
TOP TIPS FOR STRUMMING CHORDS 56
TOP TIPS FOR CONTROLLING NOTE OR CHORD DURATION 57
   21. *Away in a Manger* 58
   22. *Once in Royal David's City* 59
   23. *God Rest Ye Merry Gentlemen* 60
   24. *The Nutcracker March* 62
   25. *Hallelujah Chorus (from Handel's Messiah)* 64
SONGS WITH NOTES ON THE 5 LOWER STRINGS (A , D , G , B , E)
   26. *Here We Come A'Caroling* 66
   27. *Dance of the Sugar Plum Fairies* 68
   28. *Silent Night* 70
   29. *We Wish You a Merry Christmas* 71
   30. *The 12 Days of Christmas* 72
TOP TIPS FOR IMPROVING LEFT HAND DEXTERITY AND SPEED 74
FRETBOARD LABELS 75
COMPLETION CERTIFICATE 80

Hi Kids! My name is **Alan**. I'm going to teach you how to play music. Using my awesome system, you don't need to know anything fancy or technical—all you need is to know your colors, be able to follow a tune, and maybe even sing along. It's easy! Once you learn my cool, color-coded system, you'll be able to play a bunch of songs you probably already recognize, just by pressing the colors on the fretboard. Let's play!

Unsure what a song should sound like? Don't worry! We've collected all the songs in one place so you can listen to them!

Just scan this QR code, and any time you see this symbol:

find the corresponding letter or number and hit "download" to hear the song!

Introduction to the Guitar

Congratulations on your new guitar! We're going to have so much fun learning to play. Let's start by learning the parts of the guitar as shown in the diagram below.

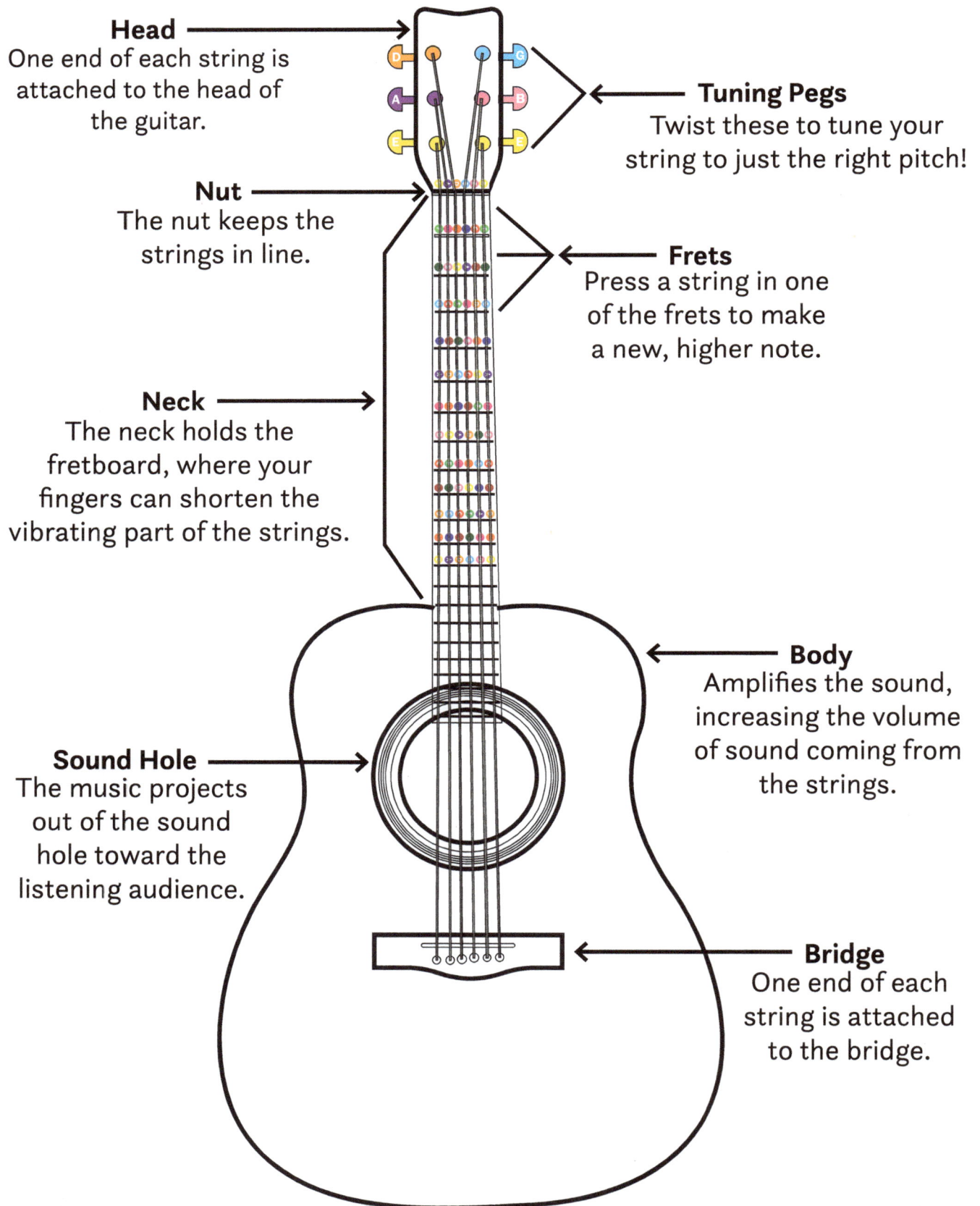

Head
One end of each string is attached to the head of the guitar.

Tuning Pegs
Twist these to tune your string to just the right pitch!

Nut
The nut keeps the strings in line.

Frets
Press a string in one of the frets to make a new, higher note.

Neck
The neck holds the fretboard, where your fingers can shorten the vibrating part of the strings.

Body
Amplifies the sound, increasing the volume of sound coming from the strings.

Sound Hole
The music projects out of the sound hole toward the listening audience.

Bridge
One end of each string is attached to the bridge.

Tuning the Strings

First things first! We start with the strings:

"Eddie Ate Dynamite, Good Bye Eddie"

There are 6 guitar strings, from **thickest at the top** to **thinnest at the bottom**. Each string is tuned to a note with a letter name.

The strings can be remembered with the acronym:

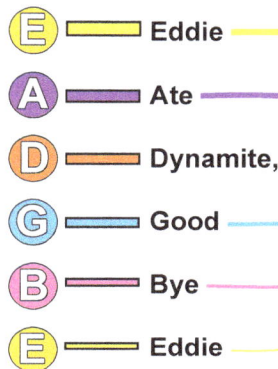

(E) — Eddie
(A) — Ate
(D) — Dynamite,
(G) — Good
(B) — Bye
(E) — Eddie

Tune your guitar with a digital headstock tuner before every session of play. This will make sure the strings sound the right notes. Start with the lowest pitch note on the thickest string, up to the highest, in the order **E-A-D-G-B-E**.

Many guitars come with a tuner and instructions, but if yours didn't, see our website for recommendations and guidance.

The tuner clips on to the head of the guitar.

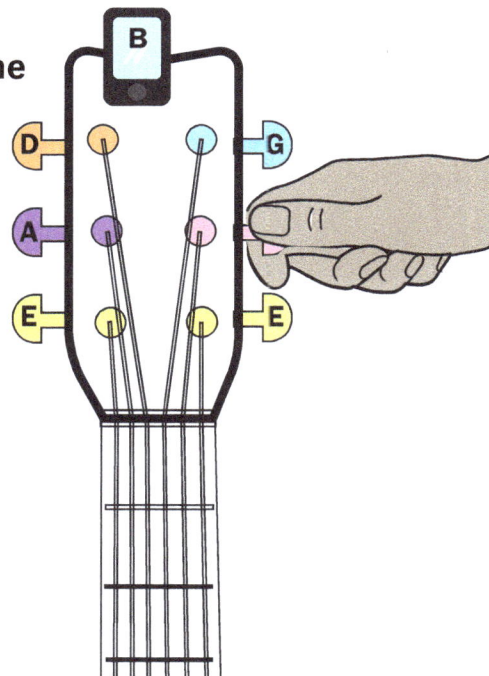

Color-Coding the Guitar

We color-code the notes in this book and on the guitar to make it easier to learn to play.

All you need to know are the rainbow colors to get started!

* Notes A B C D E F G are the natural notes, starting with the red C.
* A half-step up is called a sharp (#).
* A half-step down is called a flat (b).

C# C D Eb E F F# G G# A Bb B

Ow! That upward point is sharp!

Lie down flat to have a snooze.

Each string begins its own rainbow sequence of notes, starting with a different letter. Follow each string from left to right. Only the natural notes are labelled with a letter. **Press the string to the fretboard. This shortens the string to play a higher note.**

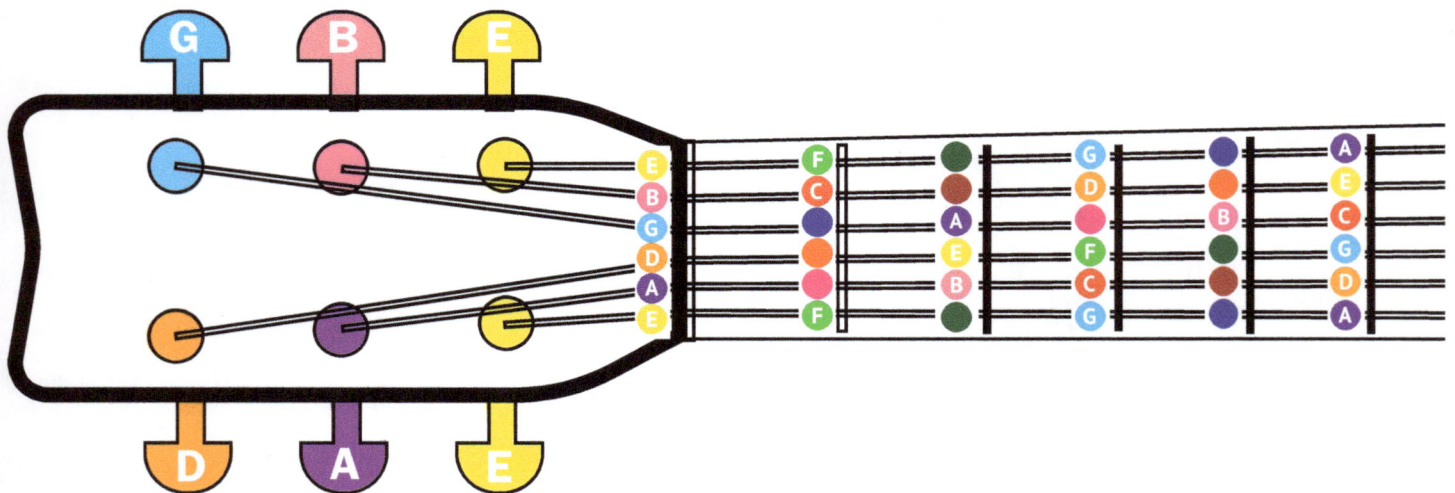

On page 75 of this book, you will find color labels for your guitar's fretboard. The labels go under the strings. They will help you match your fret fingering to the notes on the page.

Once you have set up your color-coded guitar, follow any string down the fretboard. Each fret down is a half-step note change, in the same order shown above.

Matching the TAB staff to the Guitar Strings

TAB is a staff of lines which tells you what string to play to sound a note.

When reading TAB, **imagine you've put the guitar face up on the table in front of you, with the head of the guitar on the left.** This aligns with the TAB staff as shown below.

The shape on a note tells you which finger to fret with.

G — Play an open G string, no fret (0)

C — Fret the B string in the 1st fret (1)

E — Fret the D string in the 2nd fret (2)

F — Fret the D string in the 3rd fret (3)

F# — Fret the D string in the 4th fret (4)

TAB

			Bottom string
Eddie	E		
Bye	B	1	
Good	G	0	
Dynamite	D		2 3 4
Ate	A		
Eddie	E	Top string	

GUITAR

Putting it all together...

The TAB line the note is on tells you what string to play with the right hand, and fret with the left. The color tells you what note it is. The number tells you on what fret to press the string, and the shape tells you which finger to press with.

Pluck the string to play the note.

Preparing to Play

The way you hold your body, and hold the guitar, plays a big part in how good your music sounds. New players should sit with the guitar resting on the leg below their dominant hand.

To make sounds, we strum or pluck the strings over the soundhole. The six strings are all of different lengths and widths. If you push down on one of the strings at the frets as you play it, a higher note sounds out. The vibration of the strings resonates through the body of the guitar and the sound is projected out the sound hole.

Sound complicated? Don't worry! It's actually quite simple...

1. Place this book on a music stand so your posture is upright as you read the music. Adjust the stand so you play with your back straight and your head up. This way you can avoid back and neck strain, and see your music easily.

2. The dip of the guitar rests on the upper leg on the same side as your strumming hand. Right-handed players usually rest the guitar on their right leg, just below the chest.

3. The guitar front should be angled slightly upwards, to give you a view of the fret board.

4. The elbow of your fret hand should be at an angle smaller than 90 degrees. The smaller the angle, the less strain there will be on your wrist when it is reaching around the fretboard.

5. The elbow of your strumming arm should be at the top corner of the body of the guitar.

6. Cradle the upper part of the guitar neck between your thumb and the four fingers of your fret hand. The thumb rests lightly at the top of the neck or behind it.

Your left hand presses the strings to the fretboard...

...while your right hand plucks or strums the strings.

Left Hand on Fretboard

Right Hand over the Body

Playing Notes

Let's start by playing different notes on the same string.

Play the first string open, then press the string down in the 1st fret and play the same string. Step down the fretboard with the next finger on each next fret. Each note in TAB shows you which finger of your left hand to use to fret the note. The hand diagram below the TAB staff shows what string to play and where to fret. The number is the fret in which you press the string.

The high E string.

0   1   2 — **Bottom** string — 3

"2" = 2nd fret

Top string

	1st Fret	2nd Fret	3rd Fret
E	F	F#	G

The B string.   The G string.

Bottom string –

0   1   2   3   0   1   2   3

Top string

	1st Fret	2nd Fret	3rd Fret		
B	C	C#	D	G	G#

The D string.   The A string.   The low E string.

0   1   2   3   0   1   2   3   0   1   2   3

D D# E F   A Bb B C   E F F# G

NOTE: **0 0 0 0** and **0** are all open notes, where no strings are pressed at a fret.

The bottom 3 lines of the TAB staff are darkened to show the heavier, copper-wound strings.

Note Timing and Note Length

4 The Time Signature, Notes and Measures

The Time Signature tells us how to count time. The top number tells us how many beats are in a measure. The note below it tells you what kind of note gets one beat. This time signature tells us there are 4 beats in a measure, and a quarter note gets one best.

The TAB staff is divided by vertical lines. The space between a pair of vertical lines is called a measure. This is a unit of time, made up of a number of beats, shown in the top number of the time signature.

beats per measure.

1 measure

Up   on the house-top   rein-deer pause,   out jumps good   old   San - ta Claus.

Note which gets 1 beat.

Below the staff are the **Note Stems**. The stems tells you how long to hold the note for (see below).

Note stems tell you how long to hold the note

Time duration of note stems:

An **Eighth Note** is held for 1/2 beat.	A **Quarter Note** is held for **1** beat.	A **Dotted Quarter Note** is held for **1.5** beats.	A **Half Note** is held for **2 beats**.	A **Dotted Half Note** is held for **3 beats**.	A **Whole Note** is held for **4 beats**.

To stop the string or strings from vibrating, roll your strumming hand to the right so the side of your palm pushes lightly on all the strings at once, over the soundhole. This will mute the strings.

Don't worry if you don't get all this at first! It will take a few practice sessions to feel comfortable with your new instrument.

Strumming Chords 🔊

Guitarists play notes (one string at a time), and strum chords (many strings together). **Learn to play the notes of the songs in this book first, then go through the book again and learn to strum the chords.**

To play a chord, first set your fingers to the fretboard. These are some chords you will find in this book:

The **black shapes** tell you which fingers, on which strings, and in which fret.

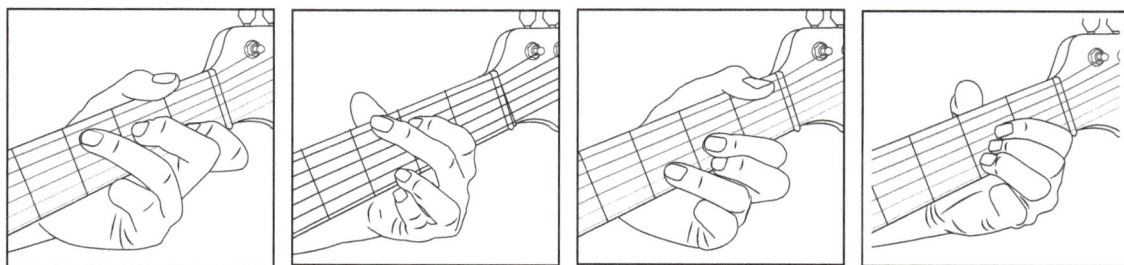

Reading a Chord Chart

A sample chord chart is shown below.

The chord chart is a vertical version of the guitar's upper fretboard. Imagine turning the chord chart clockwise 90 degrees as below. This shows you the frets to play and which fingers to use.

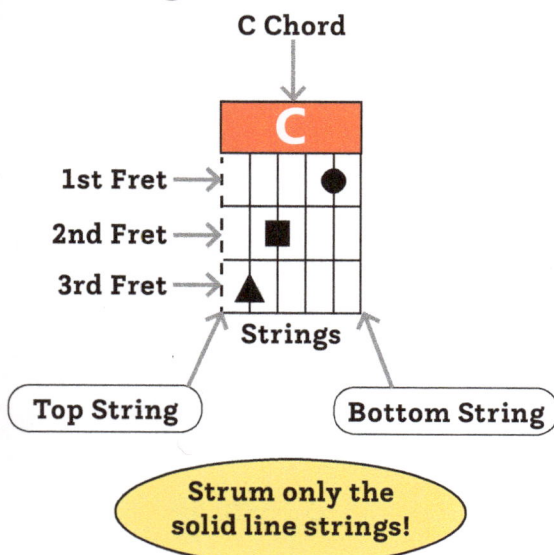

C Chord

1st Fret →
2nd Fret →
3rd Fret →

Strings

Top String
Bottom String

Strum only the solid line strings!

Strumming Patterns and Time

Strumming is playing many strings together in downstrokes and upstrokes with the right hand. You should use a guitar pick to get the right sound.

Always clap out the strumming pattern first.

This will help you avoid an awkward tangle-up!

Read: **"One..... Two-and, Three..., Four-and"**

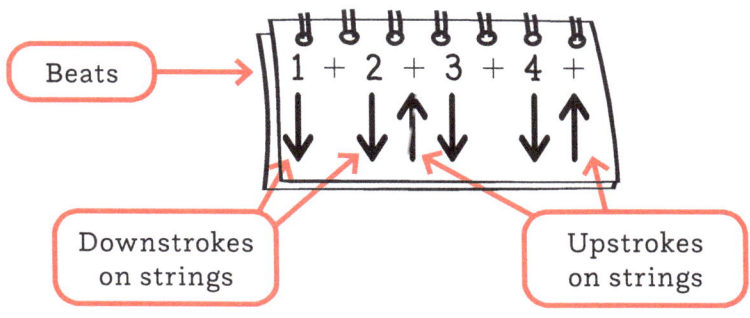

Beats →

1 + 2 + 3 + 4 +

Downstrokes on strings

Upstrokes on strings

Clap out the strumming patterns below. When you encounter a new pattern, clap it out first and practice it repeatedly until it feels relaxed and easy.

3

3.1 1 + 2 + 3 + ↓

3.2 1 + 2 + 3 + ↓ ↓ ↓

3.3 1 + 2 + 3 + ↓ ↓ ↓↑

3.4 1 + 2 + 3 + ↓ ↓↑↓↑

4

4.1 1 + 2 + 3 + 4 + ↓

4.2 1 + 2 + 3 + 4 + ↓ ↓

4.3 1 + 2 + 3 + 4 + ↓ ↓ ↓ ↓

4.4 1 + 2 + 3 + 4 + ↓ ↓↑↓ ↓↑

This is the **bottom** string

This is the **top** string

3rd Fret   D

1st Fret   C

2nd Fret   A

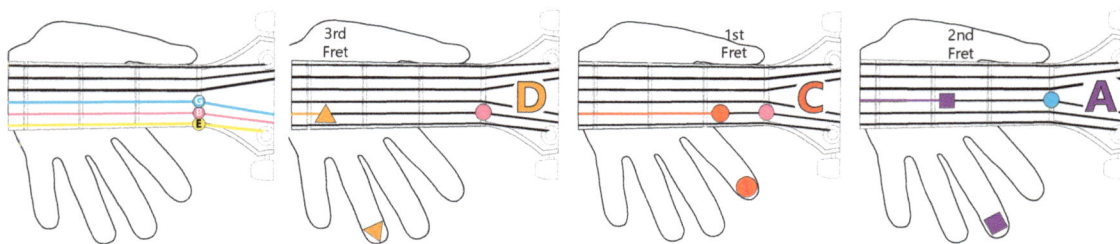

1. Up On the Housetop

| G | | C | D7 |

Up   on the house–top   rein–deer pause,   out jumps good old   San – ta Claus.

| G | | C | D7 |

Down through the chim–ney with lots   of   toys,   all   for the lit–tle ones' Christ–mas joys.

Ho, ho, ho, who would-n't go? Ho, ho, ho, who would-n't go——?

Up on the house–top, click, click, click, down through the chim–ney with good Saint Nick.

*Play the G chord in this measure as a different strumming pattern to end the song.

Bottom string

Top string

3rd Fret — **G**

1st Fret — **F**

3rd Fret — **D**

1st Fret — **C**

2nd Fret — **A**

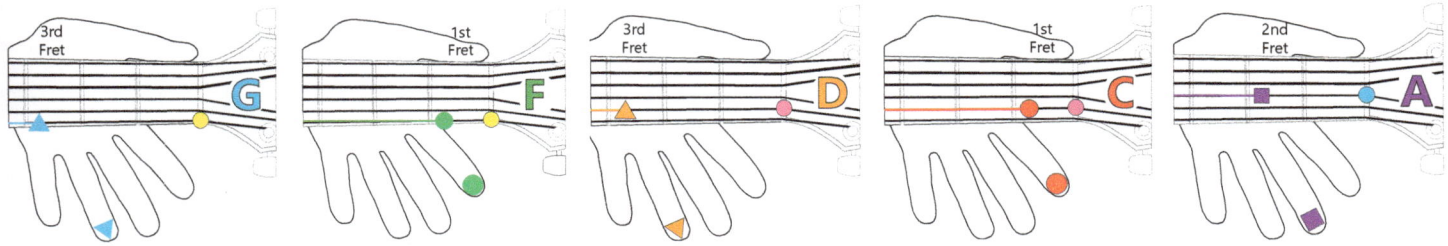

2. Good King Wenceslas

1 + 2 + 3 + 4 +

C   G   C

Good King Wen-ces - las looked out   on   the   feast   of   Ste - phen,

G   C

when the snow lay round a bout, deep and crisp and e – ven.

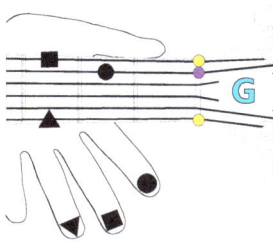

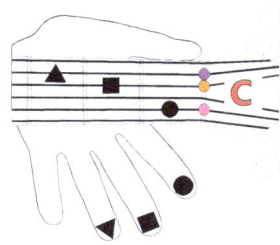

Bright – ly shone the moon that night, though the frost was crust – ed,

when a poor man came in sight, gath'ring win – ter fu – el.

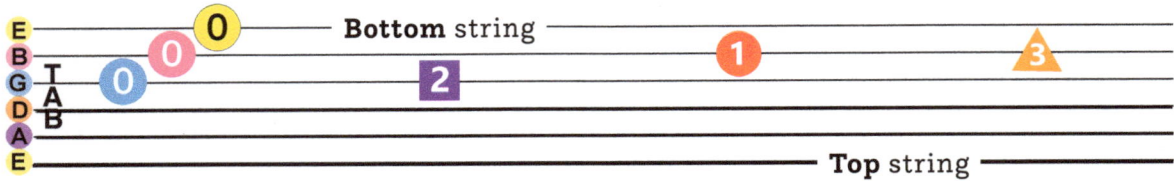

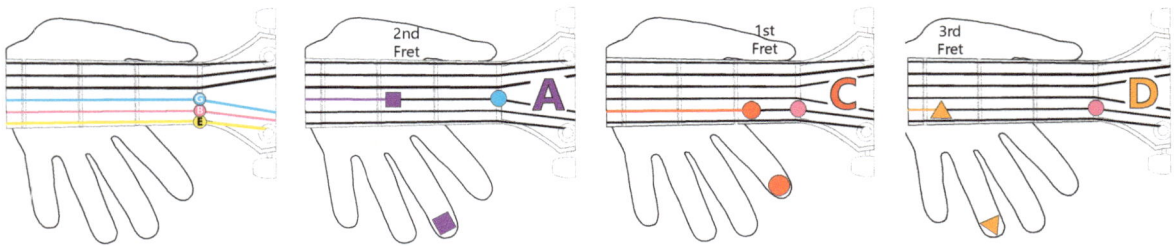

3. Jolly Old Saint Nicholas

Jol – ly   old   Saint   Nich – o – las,   lean   your   ear   this   way.

Don't   you   tell   a   sin – gle   soul   what   I'm   going   to   say.

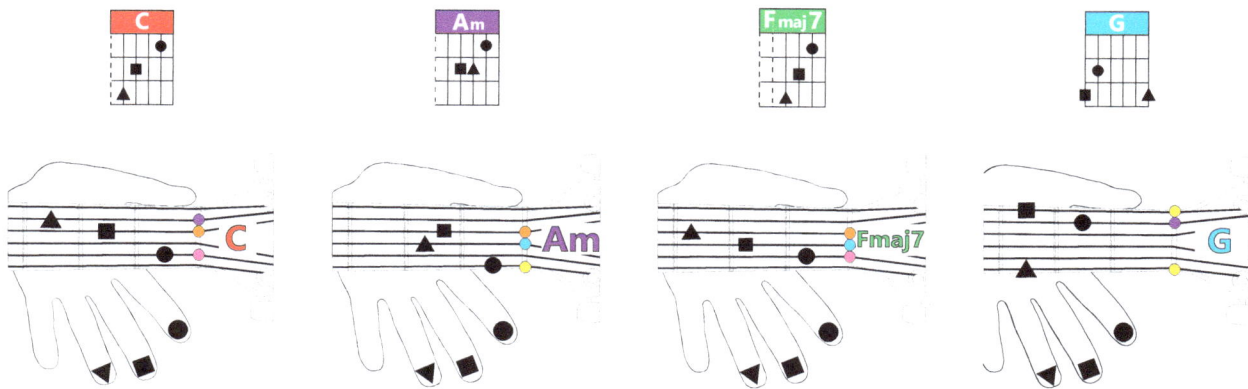

C

E	0 0 0 0			
B G D A E (TAB)		**3 3 3**	**1 1 1 1**	0

Christ – mas Eve is com – ing soon; now, you dear old man,

Fmaj7 · · · **C** · · · **G** · · · **C**

E		1	3 1 3 0	
B G D A E (TAB)	2 2 2 2	0 0		1

whis – per what you'll bring to me. Tell me if you can.

4. We Three Kings of Orient Are

| We | three | kings | of | O - ri - ent | are; | Bear - ing | gifts, | we |

| tra - verse | a - far, | field | and | foun - tain, | Moor | and | Mount - ain, |

Am · **G** · **C**

| fol - low - ing | yon - der | star. | Oh,——— | star | of | won - der, | star | of |

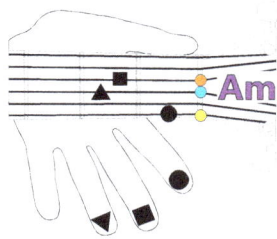
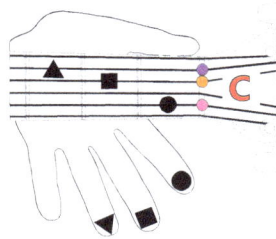
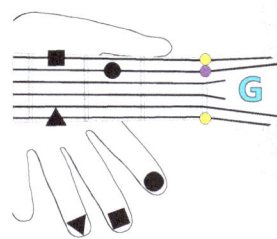
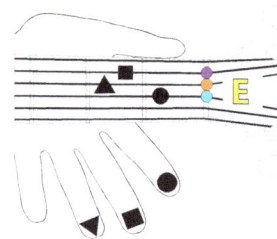

might, star with roy – al beau – ty bright, west – ward lead – ing,

still pro – ceed ing, guide us to thy per – fect light.

5. Joy to the World

Joy to the world! The Lord is come. Let earth re – ceive her

King! Let ev – e – r – y hea – r – t pre – pa – re Hi – m ro – o – m, and

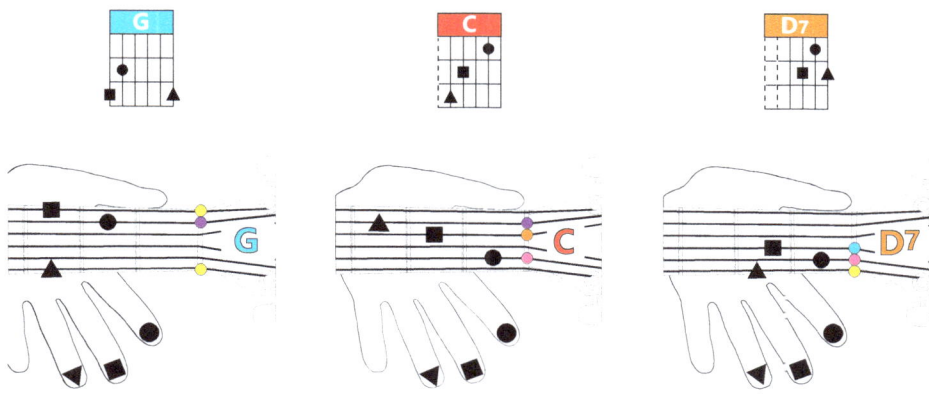

2nd Fret ... E
4th Fret ... F#
2nd Fret ... A
1st Fret ... C
3rd Fret ... D

6. Hark! The Herald Angels Sing

6

G   D   G

Hark! the her – ald an – gels si – ng, "Glo – ry to the new–born King!

D

Peace on earth, and mer – cy mi – ld, God and sin – ners re – con–ciled."

C   D

Joy – ful all ye na – tions ri – se, join the tri – umph of the ski – es;

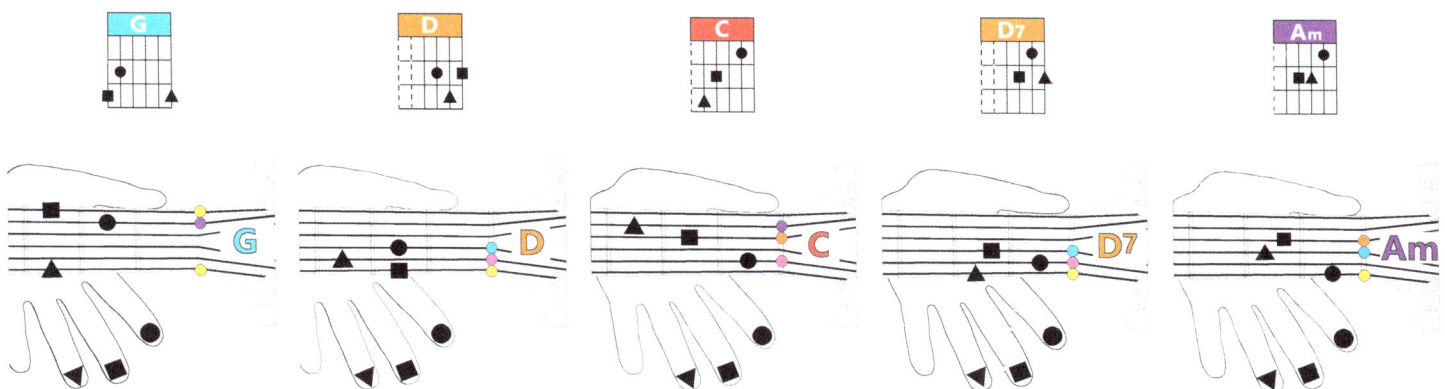

With an – gel – ic host pro – claim, "Christ i – s born in Beth – le – hem!

Hark! the her – ald an – gels sing, "Glo – r – y to the new–born King!"

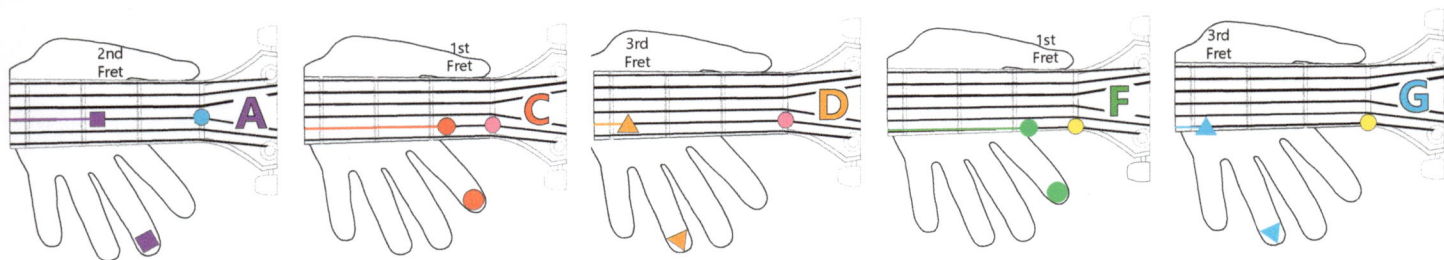

7. O Come, All Ye Faithful

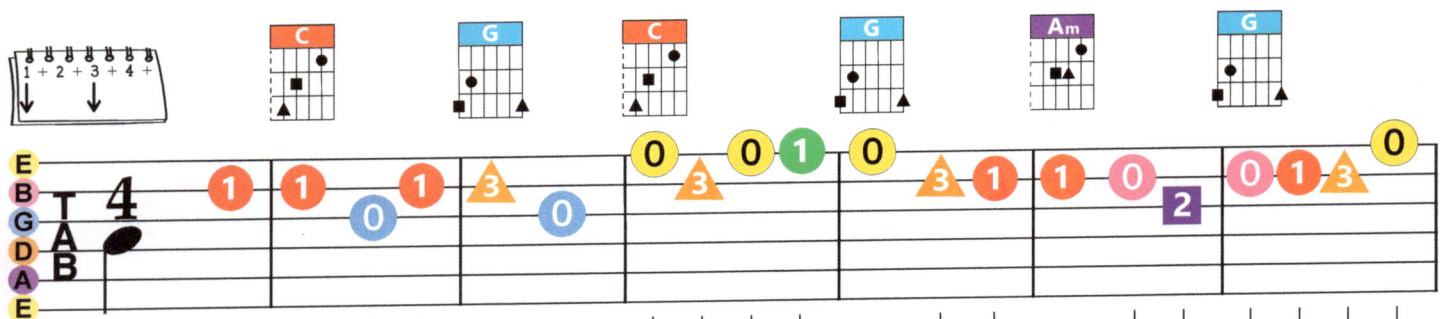

O come, all ye faith-ful, joy-ful and tri-umph-ant, O come ye, O co-me ye to

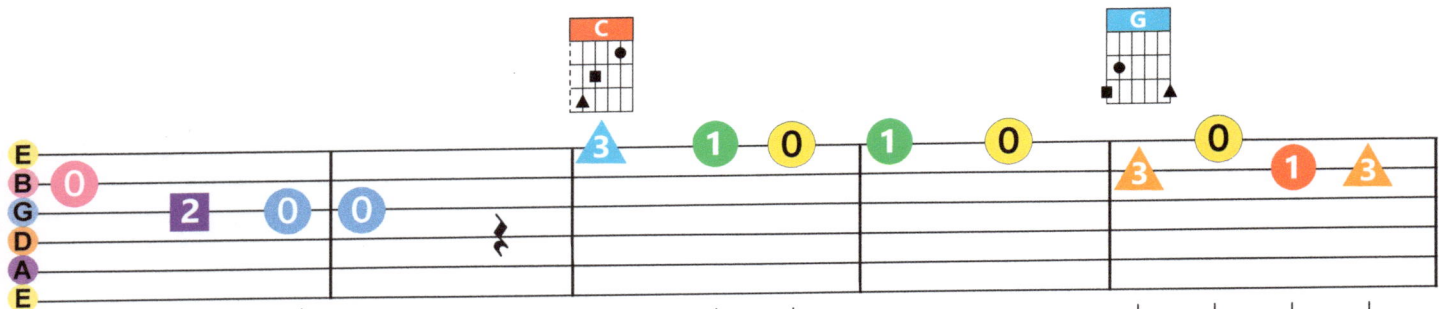

Be - th - le-hem. Come and be - hold Him, born the King of

𝄽 = 1 beat

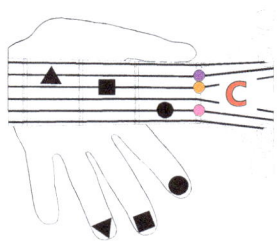

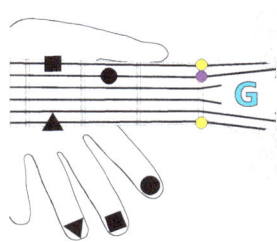

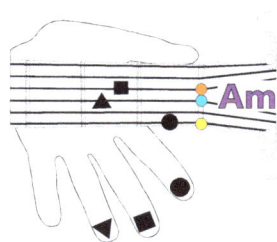

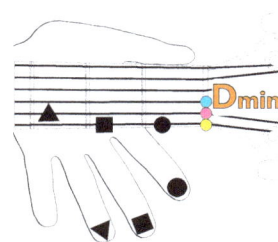

Lyrics under the tablature:

An – gels. O come, let us a – dore Him; O come, let us a –

dore Him; O come, let us a – dore Hi – m, Chri – st the Lord.

8. The First Noel

The First — No – el the — an – gels did say was to

cer – tain poor shep-herds in fields as they lay. In fields where they

lay keep – ing — their sheep on a cold win – ter's ni – ght that

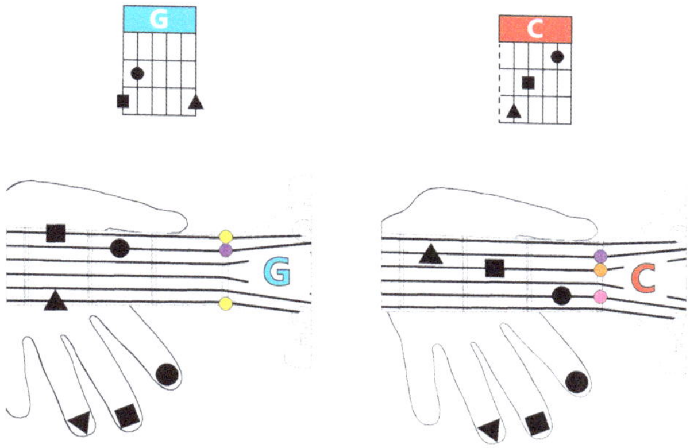
G
C
G
C

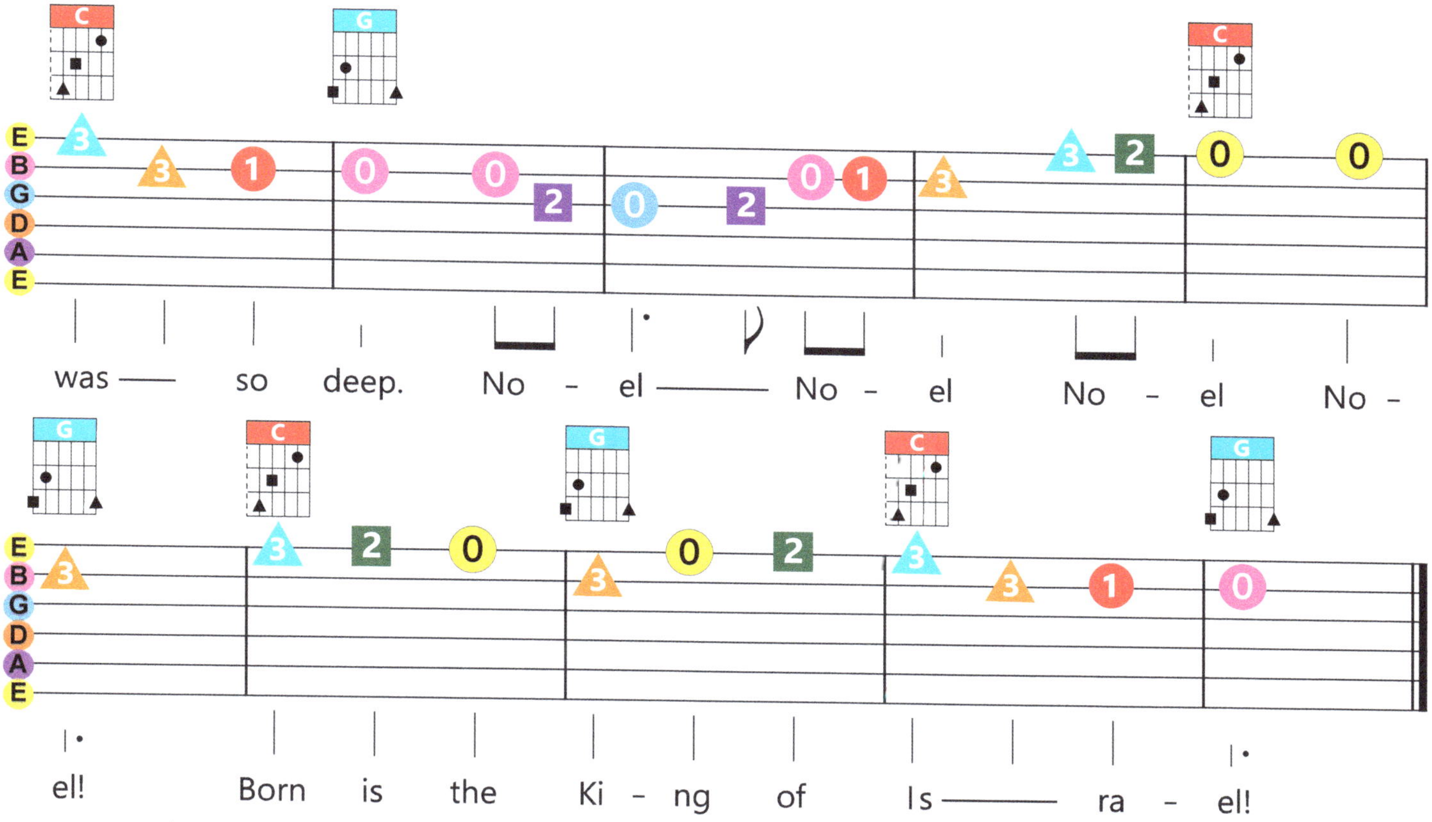
C G C
E B G D A E
was — so deep. No - el — No - el No - el No -
G C G C G
E B G D A E
el! Born is the Ki - ng of Is — ra - el!

Tip Break!
Top Tips for Playing Notes

1. Practice playing the notes in the song first.

Look at the notes in the diagrams above the song, and practice playing those notes, and moving between those notes. This will get you warmed up to play the new tune.

2. Clap out the rhythm of the song before you play it.

You probably know a lot of the songs in this book already, but for any you don't know, clap through the song using the note-stem line, so you know how long to hold each note for.

3. Learn to play each song in sections.

You won't be able to look at the music, and the guitar, at the same time. It's easier if you learn to play a few notes at a time, practice the series and memorize how to play the phrase, then move on to the next section.

Tip Break!
Top Tips for Fretting

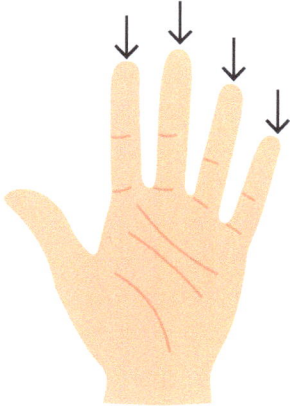

1. Fret with the tip of the finger, not the side or pad.

The strings are close together. Press the strings with the top of your finger, so you don't accidentally press other strings. Your hand and fingers will curl around the fretboard in a C shape.

2. Press the string near the metal fret.

This will create the best sound on your strings when you pluck or strum, you won't have to push as hard on the string, and it will minimize finger pain as you get started with guitar.

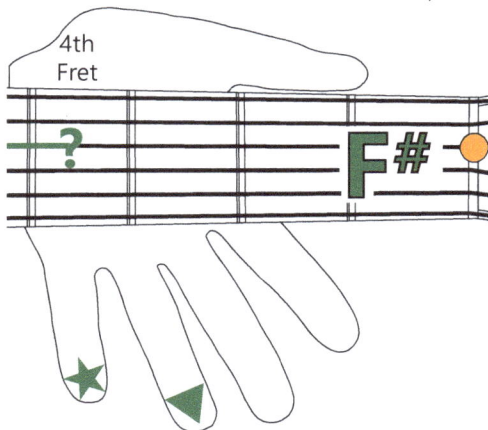

3. Use the finger that works best for you.

Some people prefer to use the ring finger in the fourth fret, some prefer the pinky. It depends how much your hand can stretch, how strong your fingers are, and when you feel comfortable moving your whole hand up and down the fretboard. Your fingers will get stronger the more you play and your hands grow, so you may change how you fret notes over time.

4th Fret

F#

9. Jingle Bells

Dashing through the snow in a one horse open sleigh, o'er the fields we

go, laugh-ing all the way. Bells on bob – tails ring, mak-ing spir-its

bright. What fun it is to ride and sing a sleigh–ing song to – night! Oh,

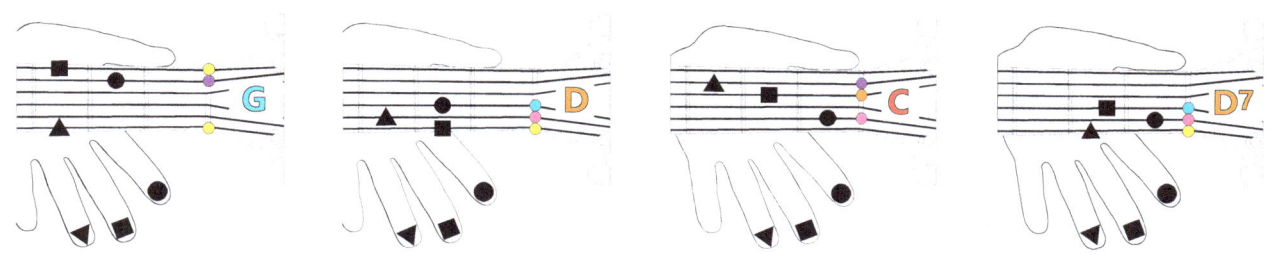

jin-gle bells,   jin-gle bells,   jin-gle all the   way!   Oh, what fun   it

is   to ride in a   one-horse o-pen   sleigh, hey!   Jin-gle bells,   jin-gle bells,

jin-gle all the   way!   Oh, what fun it   is to ride in a   one horse o-pen   sleigh!

10. Auld Lang Syne

G	D7	G	C

Should auld ac-quain-tance be for-got, and nev–er brought to mind? Should

G	D7	C	G

auld ac-quain-tance be for-got, and days of auld lang syne? For

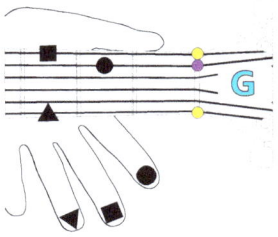

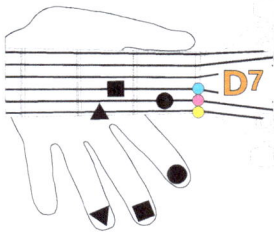

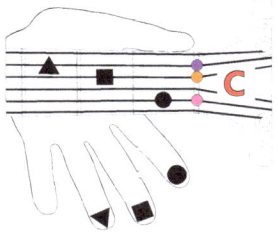

au – ld la – ng syne, my dear, for au – ld la – ng syne, we'll

take a cup o' kind – ness yet, for au – ld la – ng syne.

11. It Came Upon a Midnight Clear

11

It came up – o – n a mid – night clear, that glo – ri – ous

so – ng of old. From an – gels be – nd – ing near the

earth, to touch their ha – rps of gold. "Peace on the

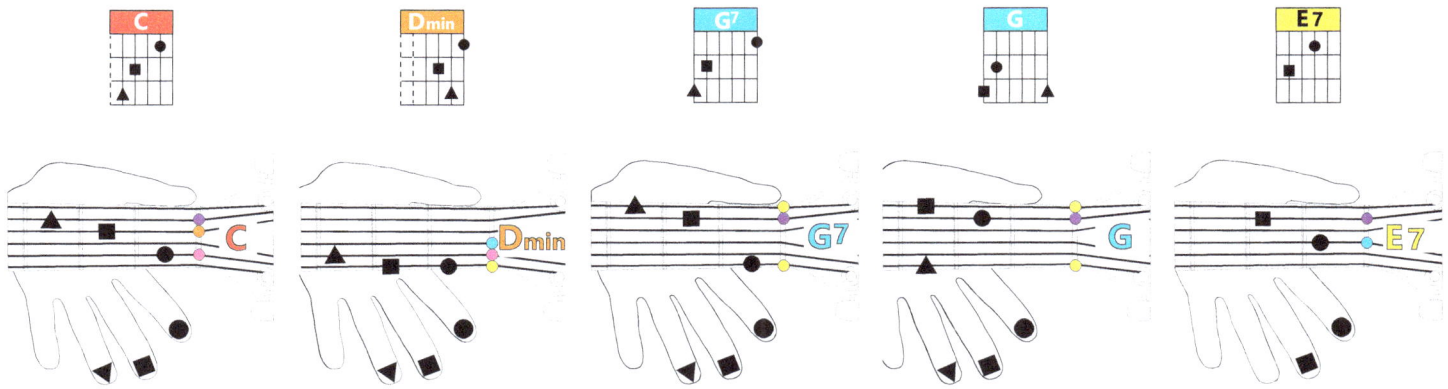

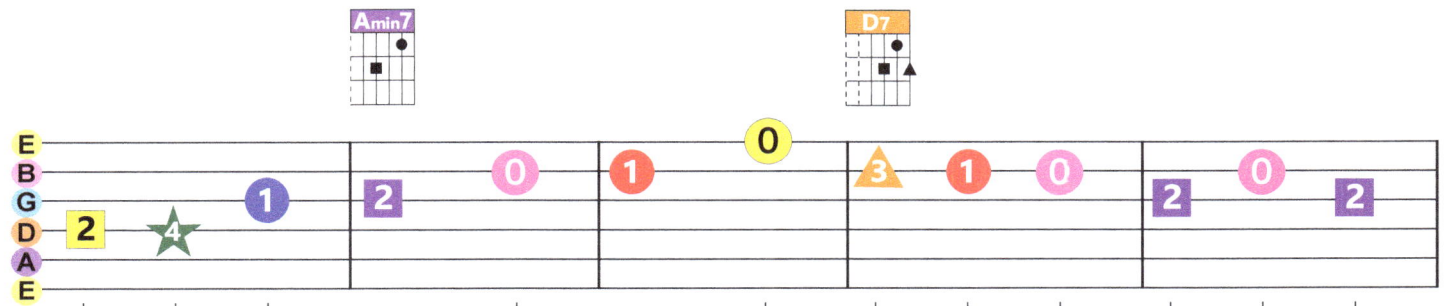

ear - th, good - will to men, from heav'n-'s al grac————ious

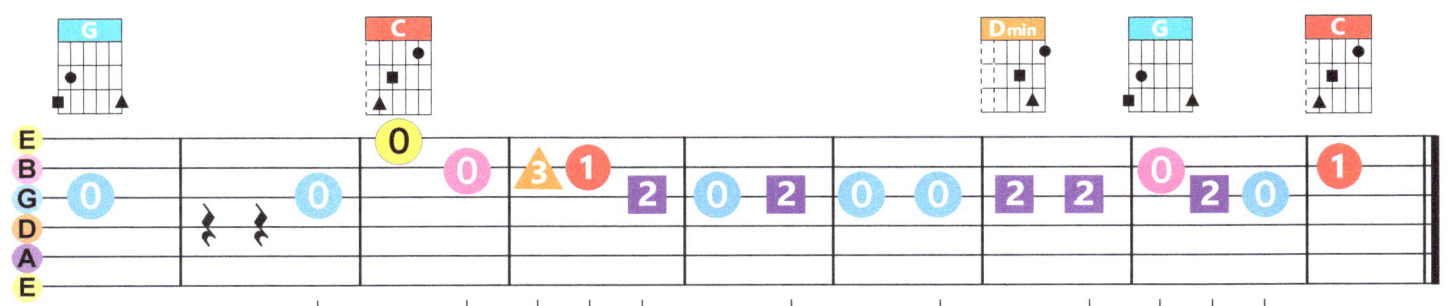

King." The world in sol - emn still-ness lay to hear the an - gels sing.

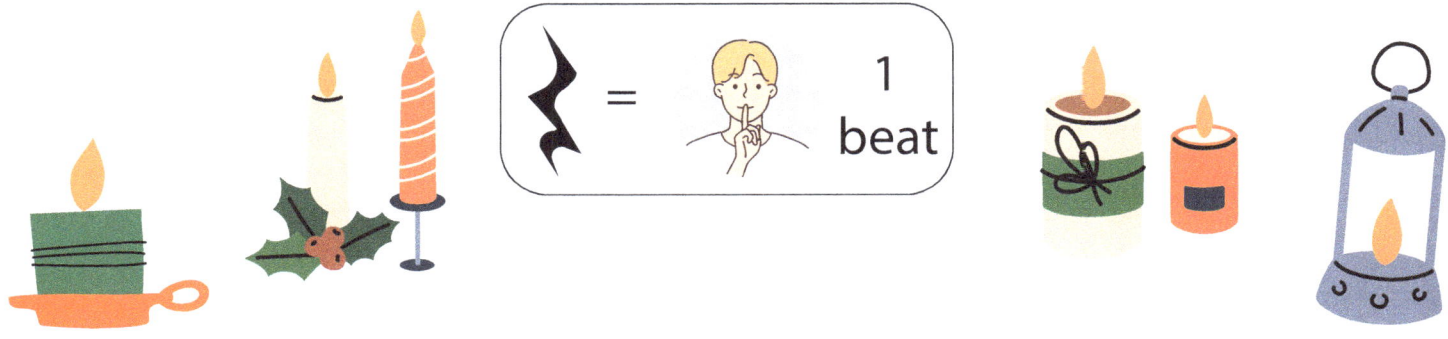

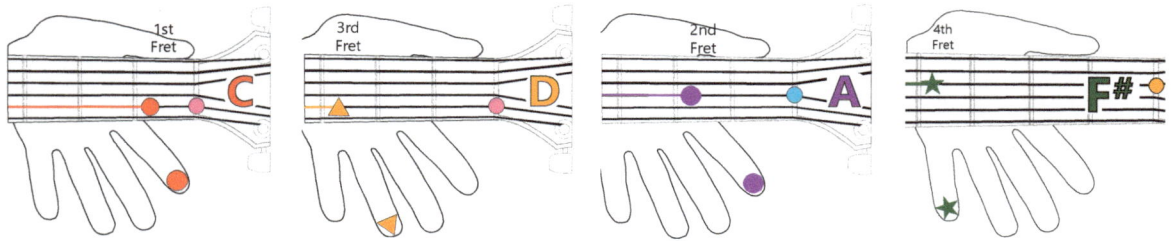

12. O Christmas Tree

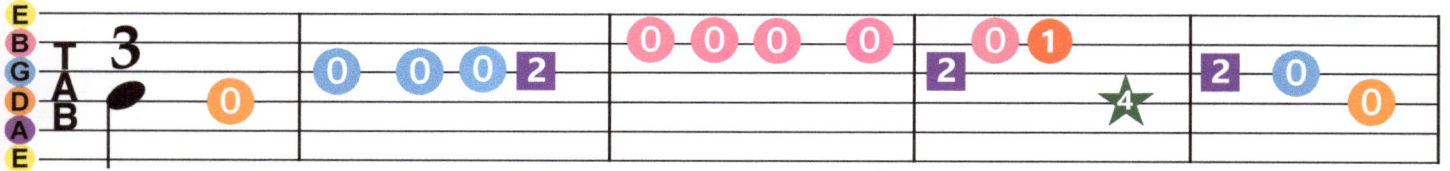

12

O Christ-mas tree, O Christ-mas tree, you stand in ver–dant beau – ty! O

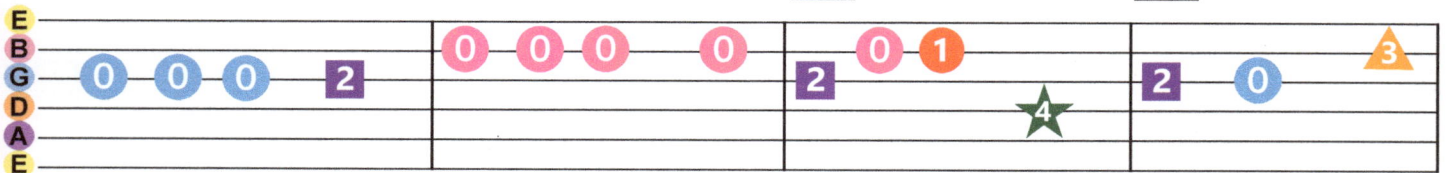

Christ-mas tree, O Christ-mas tree, you stand in ver – dant beau – ty! Your

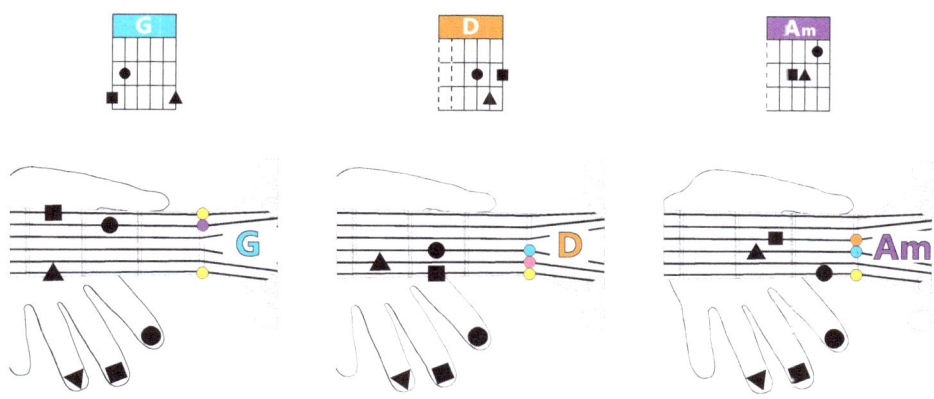

boughs are green in sum-mer's glow, and do not fade in win-ter's snow. O

Christ-mas tree, O Christ-mas tree, you stand in ver – dant beau – ty!

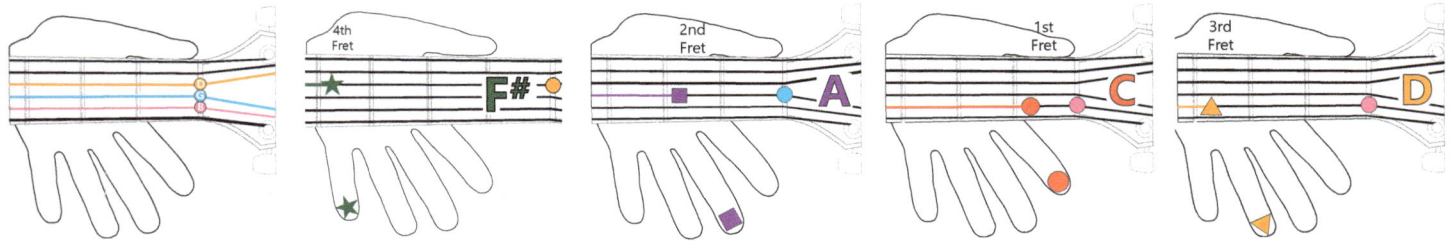

13. Gloucestershire Wassail

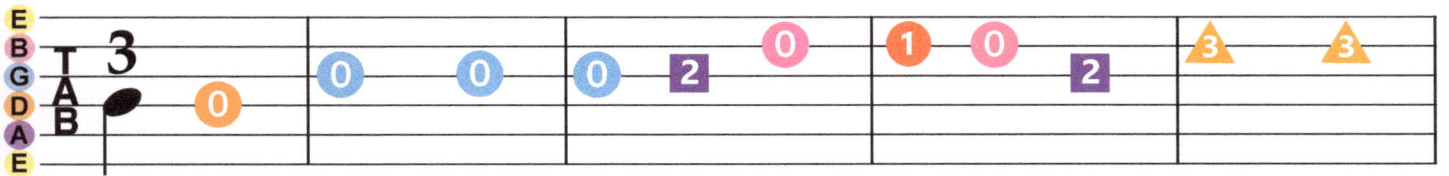

13 🔊

G   **C**   **G**

Was – sail,   was – sail,——— all   o – ver   the   town.   Our

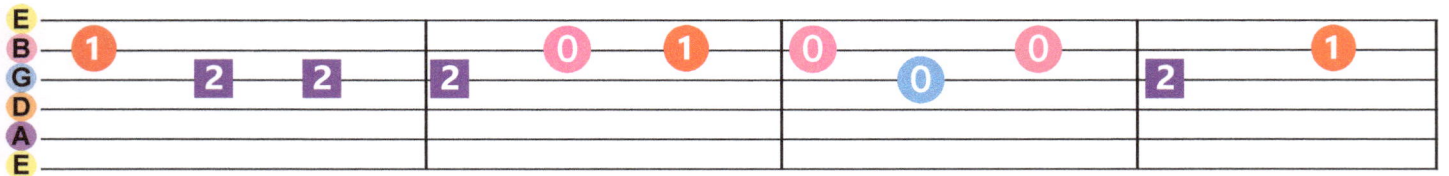

D7   **G**   **D**

toast   it   is   white,   and   our   ale   it   is   brown.   Our

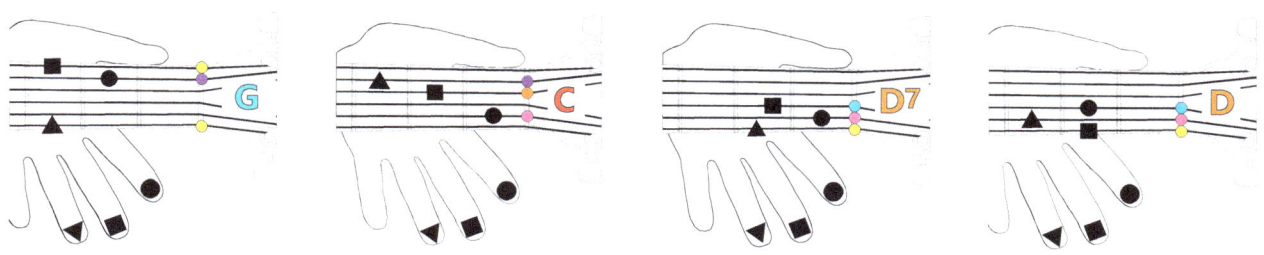

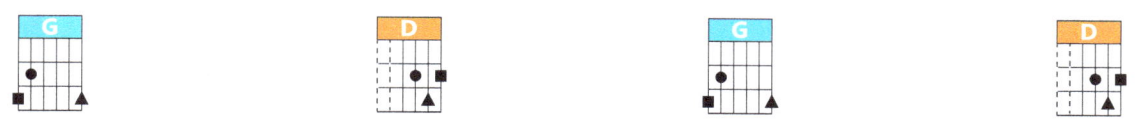

bowl   it   is   made   of   the   white   ma – ple   tree;   with the

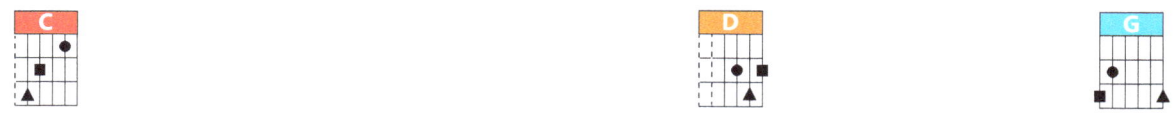

was —— sail – ing   bowl,   we'll   drink —— to   thee.

14. I Heard the Bells on Christmas Day

I heard the bells on Christ-mas day. Their old fa-mil-iar car-ols play and

mild and sweet their songs re-peat of peace on earth good-will to men.

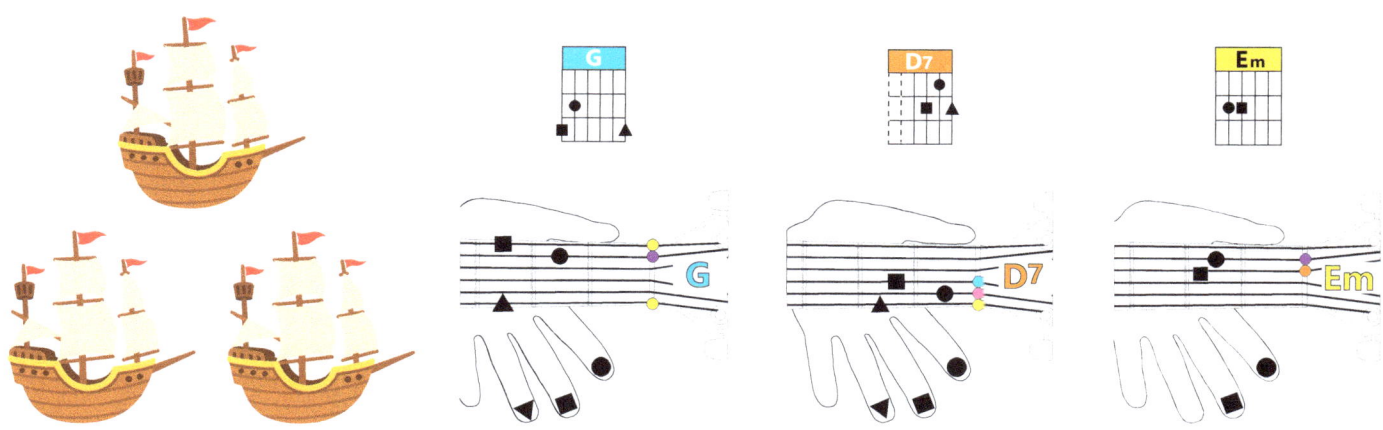

15. I Saw Three Ships

I saw three ships come sail – ing in, on Christ – mas

Day, on Christ – mas Day; I saw three ships come

sail – ing in, on Christ – mas Day in the morn – ing.

16. Deck the Halls

Deck the halls with boughs of hol – ly, Fa la la la la, la la la la.

'Tis the sea – son to be jol – ly, Fa la la la la la la la la.

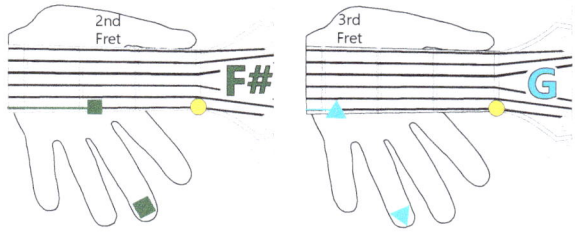

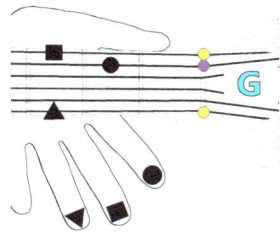

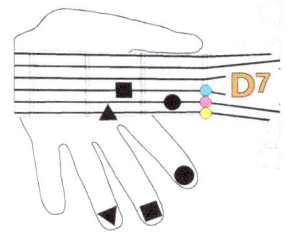

Don we now our gay ap-par – el, Fa la la, la la la, la la la.

Troll the an – cient yule-tide car – ol, Fa la la la la la la la la.

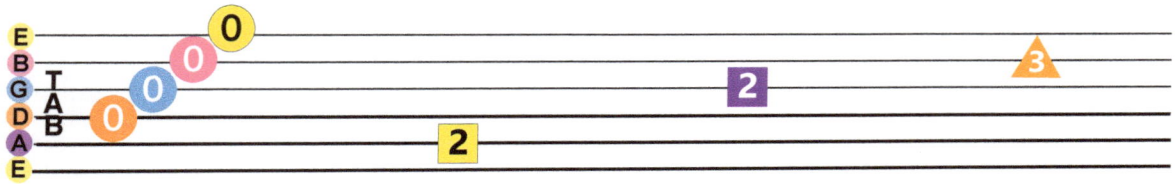

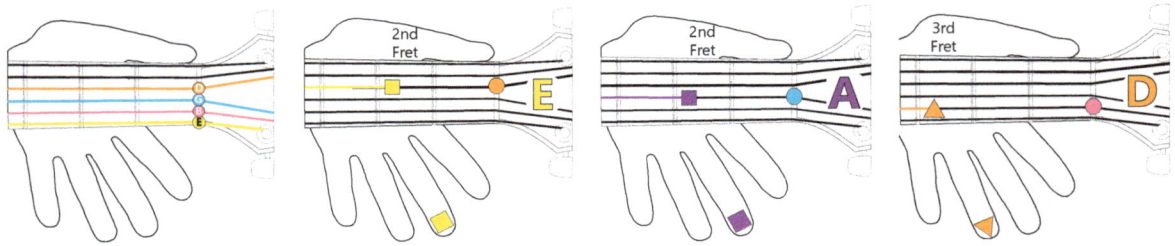

17. Go Tell It on the Mountain

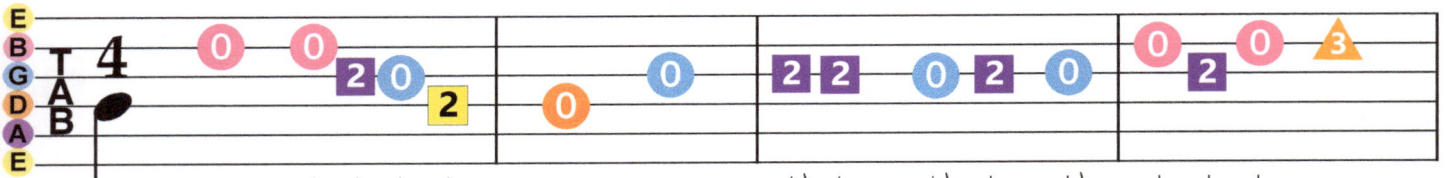

17

| 1 + 2 + 3 + 4 + |

G   D7   G   D7

Go tell it on the mount – ain o – ver the hills and ev–er–y–where.

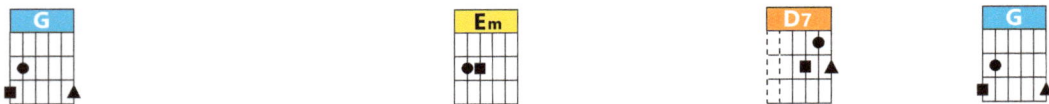

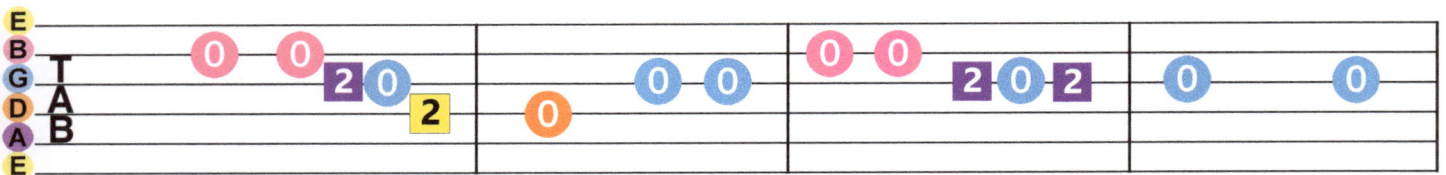

G   Em   D7   G

Go tell it on the mount – ain that Je – sus Chri-st was born. When

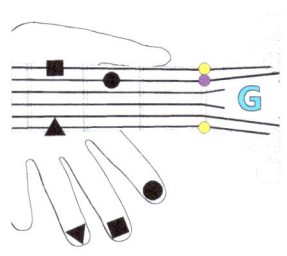
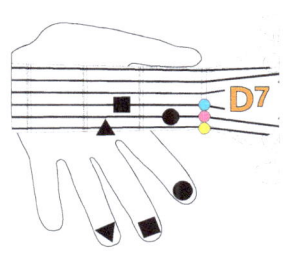
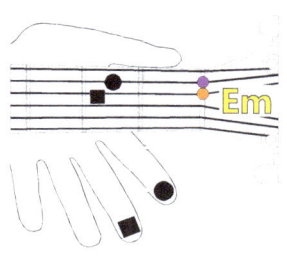

I was a see – k – er I sought both night and day. I

asked the Lord to help me and he showed me the way.

18. Angels We Have Heard on High

An-gels we have heard on high, sweet-ly sing-ing o'er the plains,

and the moun-tains in re-ply ech - o - ing their joy - ous strains.

Glo – – – – – ri – a,

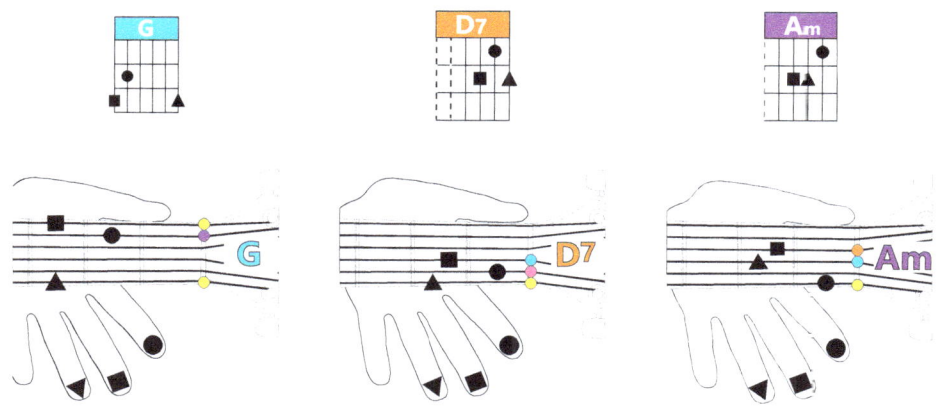

G   **D7**   **G**   **Am**

in ex – cel – sis De – o!   Glo – – –

G   **D7**   **G**   **D7**   **G**

– – ri – a,   in ex – cel – sis De – o!

19. O Little Town of Bethlehem

19 🔊

Chords: G Am G D7 G

O lit – tle town of Beth – le – hem, how still w – e see thee lie. A –

Chords: E Am G D7 G

bove thy deep and dream–less sleep, the si – le – nt stars go by. Yet

in thy dark streets shin – eth, the ev – er – last – ing light. The

hopes and fears of all the years are met in thee to – night.

20. Ding Dong Merrily on High

E — F# — A — C — D

Ding! Dong! Mer-ri-ly on high in heav'n the bells are ring-ing.

Ding dong! Ver-i-ly the sky is riv'n with an-gel sing-ing.

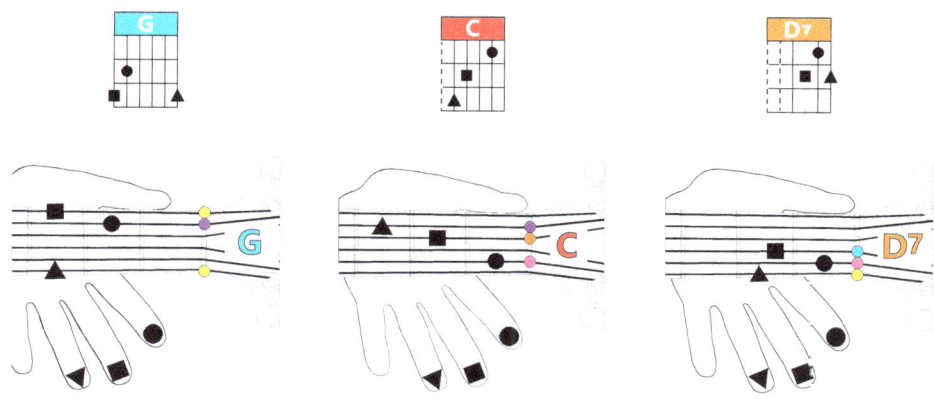

Glo – – – – – –

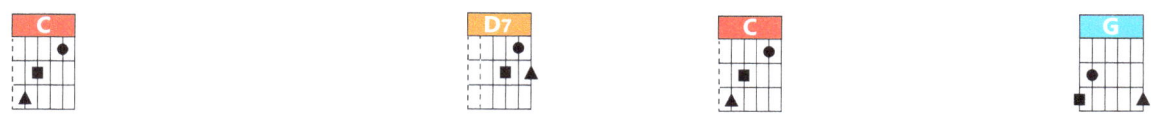

– – ri – a! Ho – san – na in ex – cel – sis!

Tip Break!

Top Tips for Strumming Chords

1. Practice chord changes.

Finger placement on the frets when changing chords can really slow down play. Practice playing each of the chords of your song first, with special attention to making quick chord changes.

Exercise: 1-minute changes

Choose 2 chords (we recommend starting with C and G). Set a stopwatch for 1 minute. See how many times you can strum each chord, by switching back and forth for one minute. Work up to 30, and aim for 60!

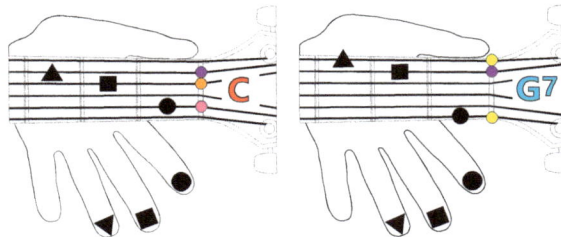

2. Practice the strumming pattern many, many times first.

- First clap out the strumming pattern 10 times.
- Second, silent-strum the pattern on your guitar 10 times. You can mute the strings by resting the side of your strumming palm on the strings while you strum.
- Thirdly, unmute the strings and strum each chord in your song with that pattern.
- Finally, play the song.

3. Learn to play each song in sections.

The same concept from playing notes applies here—you won't be able to look at the music and the guitar at the same time. Learn to play a few measures at a time, memorize the chord changes, then move on to the next section.

Tip Break!
Top Tips for Controlling Note or Chord Duration

1. Keep good time.

Gently bounce your left heel against the floor with the time signature as you play. This will help you keep time with the song and track note duration.

2. Use the side of your right hand palm to mute strings when needed.

Play notes and chords with the side of your right palm just above the strings. After plucking or strumming you can quickly mute the strings by pressing your side-palm to all strings.

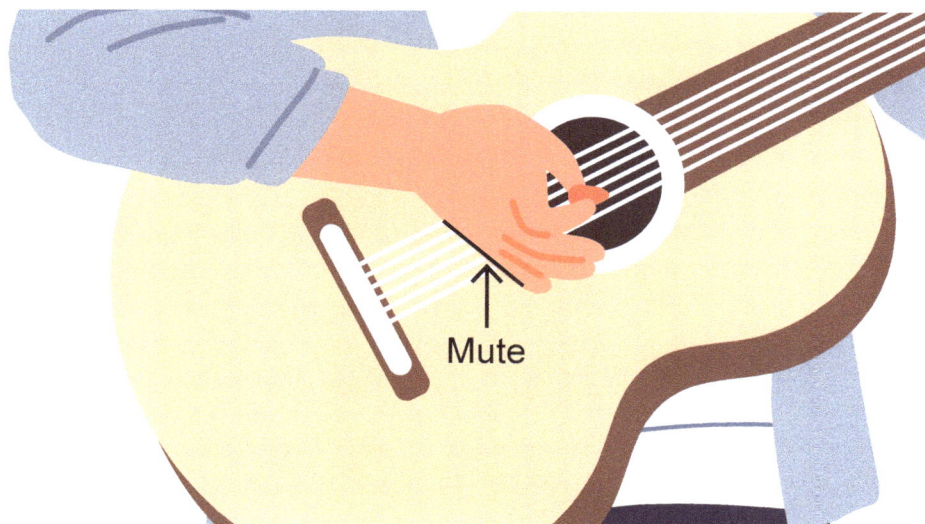

Mute

3. When playing a fast tempo, keep the strumming or plucking motion small.

One of the challenges of playing guitar is making changes with your hands quickly, to keep up with the music. Keep motions small, strong, and close to the instrument for faster play.

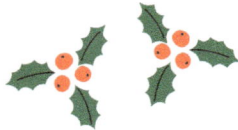

21. Away in a Manger

21 🔊

A - way in a man - ger, no crib for a bed, the

lit – tle Lord Je – sus laid down His sweet head. The stars in the sk – y look

down where He lay, the lit – tleLord Je – sus, a – sleep on the hay.

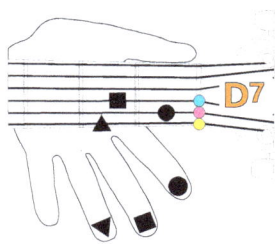

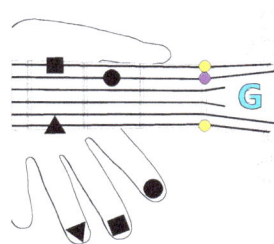

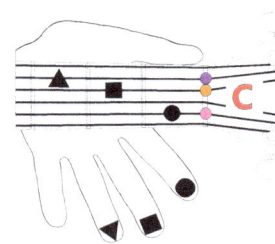

22. Once in Royal David's City

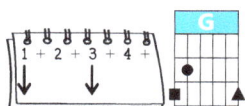

Once in Roy – al Da – vi–d's ci – ty stood a low – ly ca–tt —— le shed

where a moth – er lai–d he–r ba – by in a man – ger fo–r Hi–s bed.

Ma – ry was that moth – er mild, Je – sus Christ her li – tt —— le child.

23. God Rest Ye Merry Gentlemen

God rest ye mer - ry gen - tle - men; let noth - ing you dis - may. Re -

mem - ber, Christ our Sa - v - ior was born on Christ - mas Day to

save us all from Sa - tan's pow'r when we have gone a - stray. O——

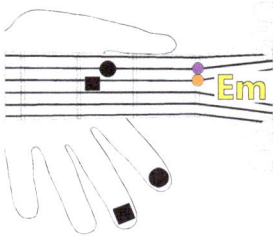 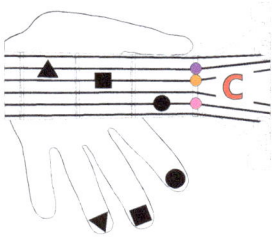 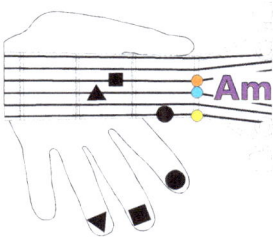 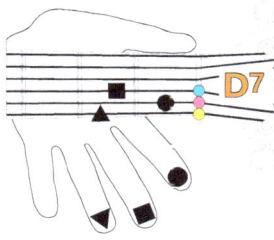 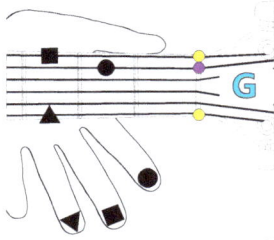

G   **Em**   **D7**

E	0	1	0	0							2	0	2
B					2	0		2	0	2			
G							4			4	2		
D													
A													
E													

tid - ings of com - fort and joy, comfort and joy! O——

G   **Em**

E	0	1	3	0	0				
B						2	0		
G								4	2
D									
A									
E									

tid ——— ings of com ——— fort and joy.

24. The Nutcracker March

25. Hallelujah Chorus

(from Handel's *Messiah*)

25 🔊

Hal – le-lu-jah! Hal – le-lu-jah! Hal-le – lu-jah! Hal-le-lu-jah! Hal–

le —— lu-jah! Hal – le - lu-jah! Hal – le - lu-jah! Hal-le-

𝄼 = ½ beat

𝄽 = 1 beat

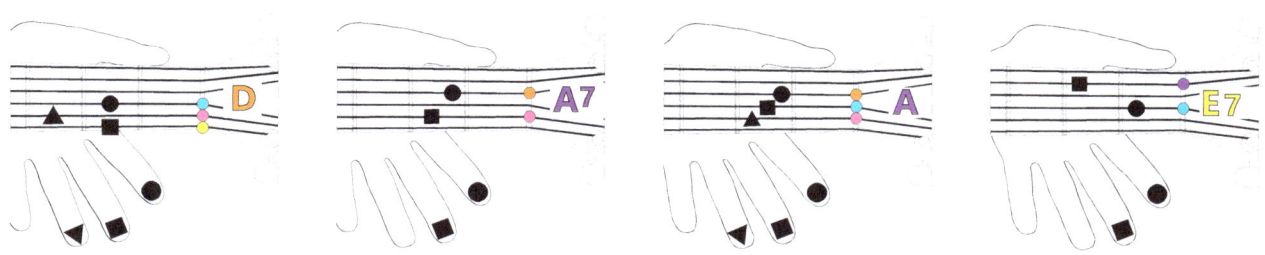

26. Here We Come A'Caroling

26

Here we come a - car - ol - ing a - mong the leaves so

green. Here we come a - wander - ing so fa - ir to be

seen. Love and joy come to you, and to you glad Christ-mas

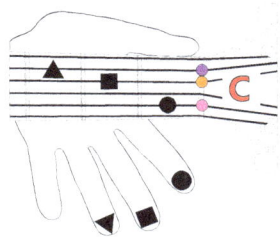 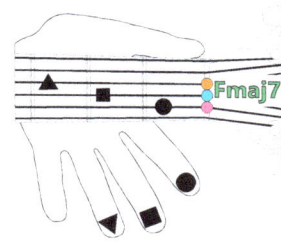 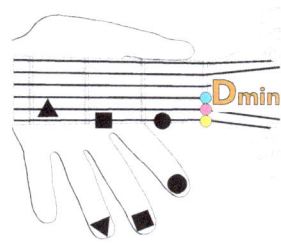 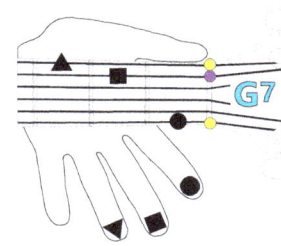

| too. | And | God | bless | you | and | se – nd | you | a | Hap – py | New |

| Year. | And | God | send | you | a | Hap – py | New | Year. |

27. Dance of the Sugar Plum Fairies

C#   C   E   B   B♭

2nd Fret   1st Fret   2nd Fret   2nd Fret   1st Fret

2.

↩ Repeat 1 time

28. Silent Night

Si——lent night! Ho——ly night! All is calm, all is bright;

Round yon Vir——gin Mo-ther and child. Ho — ly in-fant so ten-der and mild.

Sleep in heav - en-ly pea —— ce. Sleep—— in heav - en-ly peace.

29. We Wish You a Merry Christmas 29 🔊

We wish you a Mer-ry Christ-mas, we wish you a Mer-ry Christ-mas, we

wish you a Mer-ry Christ-mas and a Hap-py New Year! Good tid-ings we bring to

you and your kin; Good tid-ings for Chris-mas and a Hap-py New Year!

30. The 12 Days of Christmas

On the first day of Christ-mas, my true love gave to me a part-ri-dge in a pear

2nd, 3rd and 4th Day

tree. On the sec-ond day of Christ-mas, my true love gave to me two tur-tle doves, and a
third three fre-nch hens,
fourth four call-ing birds,

D.S. for vs 3 and 4   **5th Day**

par-tri-dge in a pear tree. On the fifth day of Christ-mas, my true love gave to me five gold-en rings, fo-ur call-ing birds, three french hens, tw-o tur-tle doves, and a

part-ri-dge in a pear tree. On the 6th day of Christ-mas, my true love gave to me
7th
8th
9th
10th
11th
12th

Six geese a——lay-ing, five gold-en rings, fo-ur call-ing birds, three french hens,
Seven swans a——swim-ming,
Eight maids a——milk-ing,
Nine la-dies danc-ing,
Ten lords a——leap-ing,
Eleven pi-pers pi-ping,
Twelve drum-mers drum-ming,

tw-o tur-tle doves, and a part-ri-dge in a pear tree.

Tip Break!
Top Tips for Improving Left Hand Dexterity and Speed

1. Do Spider Exercises.

Turn to page 12. Set each finger to a fret, and play notes up and down a string, walking with your fingers, one fret at a time. Play through 4 frets on each string, up and down the fretboard.

2. Loosen Up the Wrist.

Keep your left hand loose and active, especially as you reach for the low E and A strings at the top of the fretboard. Be ready to rotate the hand for a wider C, and move the hand back and forth along the fretboard as needed.

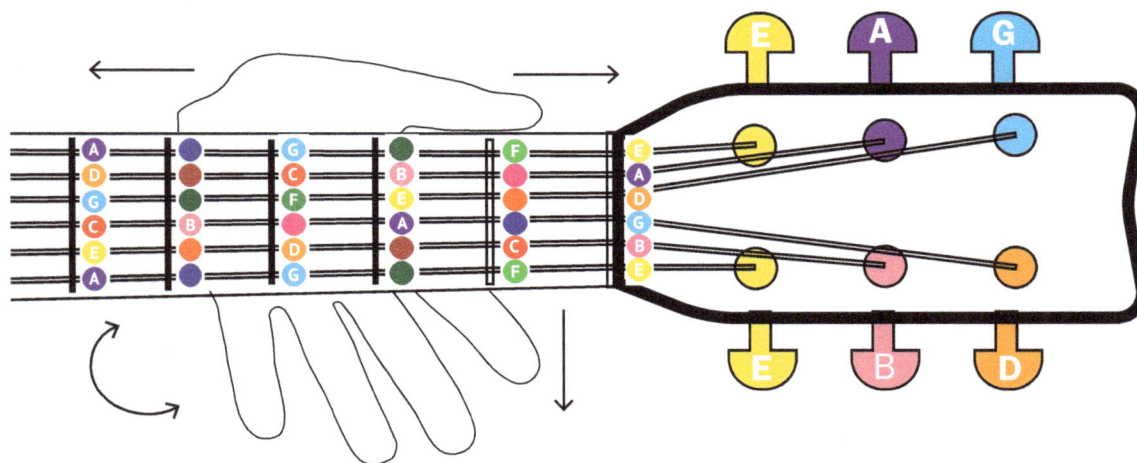

3. Try Rolling to a Finger Pad.

Where you have to play two adjacent strings in the same fret in sequence, roll the pad of your fretting finger between the two. Practice a few times before playing the song. Here's an example from "The Ten Days of Christmas":

On the first day of Christ-mas my truelovegave to me,

Fretboard Labels

You will need scissors and scotch tape!

Instructions

1. Choose a set of labels on the next page or page 79, which matches your guitar size, and cut along the white lines. You will only play notes in the first 4 frets in this book, so you can tape just those onto your guitar if you prefer. We include labels for 12 frets.

2. Run label strips beneath strings in the fret that matches the number at the bottom of the strip. Each dot should be beneath a string. See diagram below. Put the string label (0) to the left of the nut, and the 1st fret label just left of the 1st fret.

3. Fold the strip over the neck, and tape each end to the back of the guitar neck to hold the label strip in place. The label should be flat and tight to the fretboard, so tape it tightly! (A loose label may interfere with the vibration of the guitar strings.)

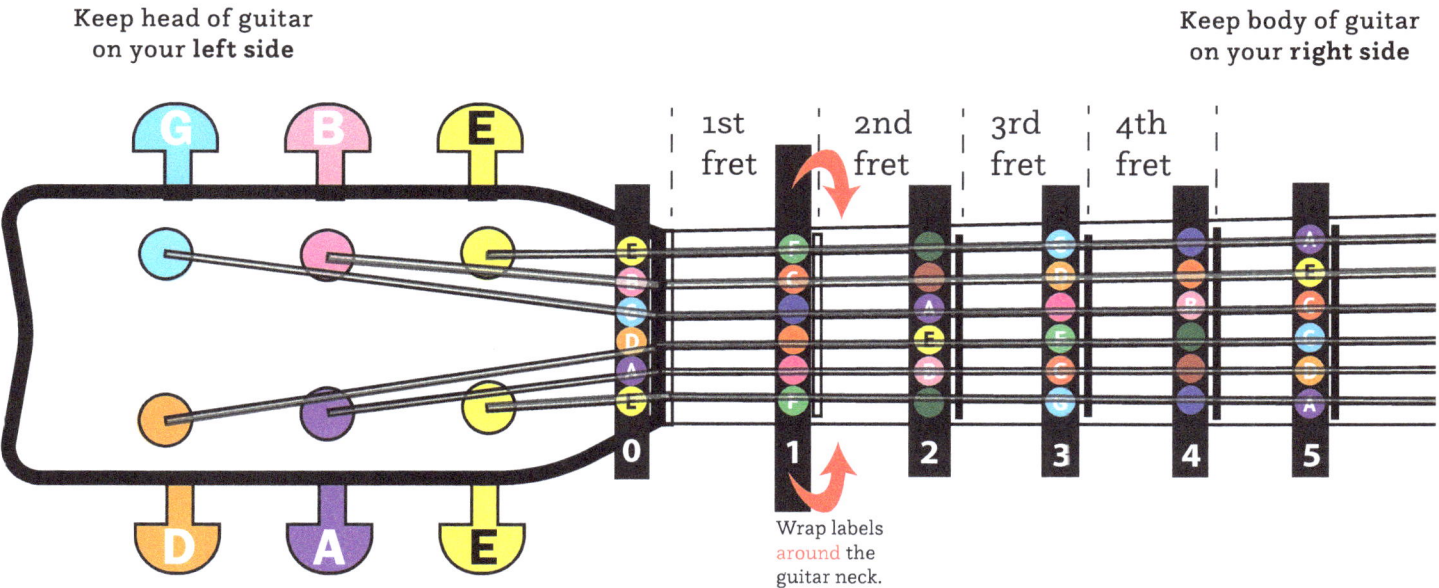

Keep head of guitar on your **left side**

Keep body of guitar on your **right side**

1st fret 2nd fret 3rd fret 4th fret

0 1 2 3 4 5

Wrap labels around the guitar neck.

Full Size Electric Guitar (Age 12+)
Full Size Narrow-Neck Acoustic
1/2 Size Acoustic (Age 5–8)

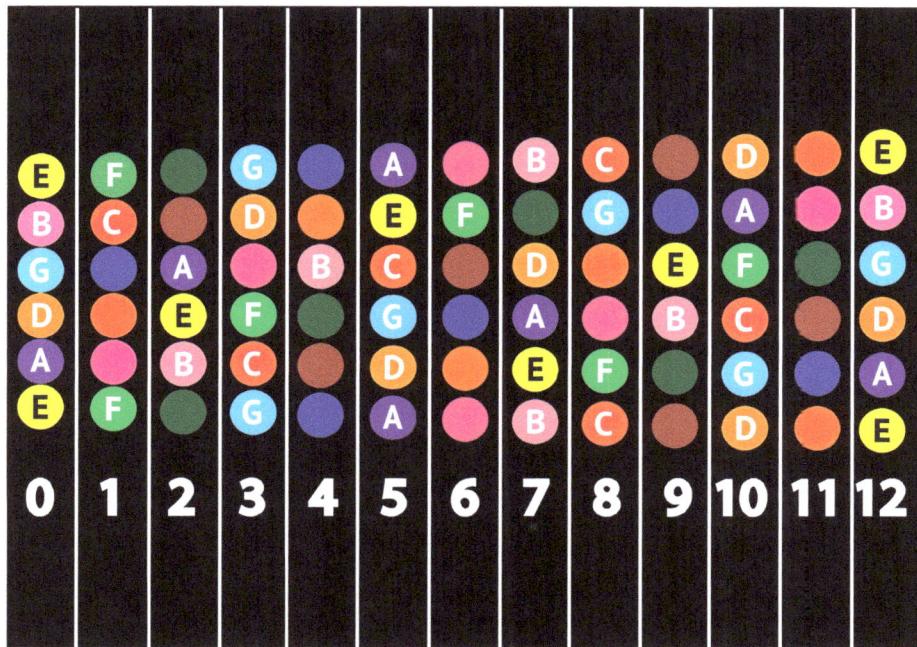

3/4 Size Acoustic (Age 8–12)

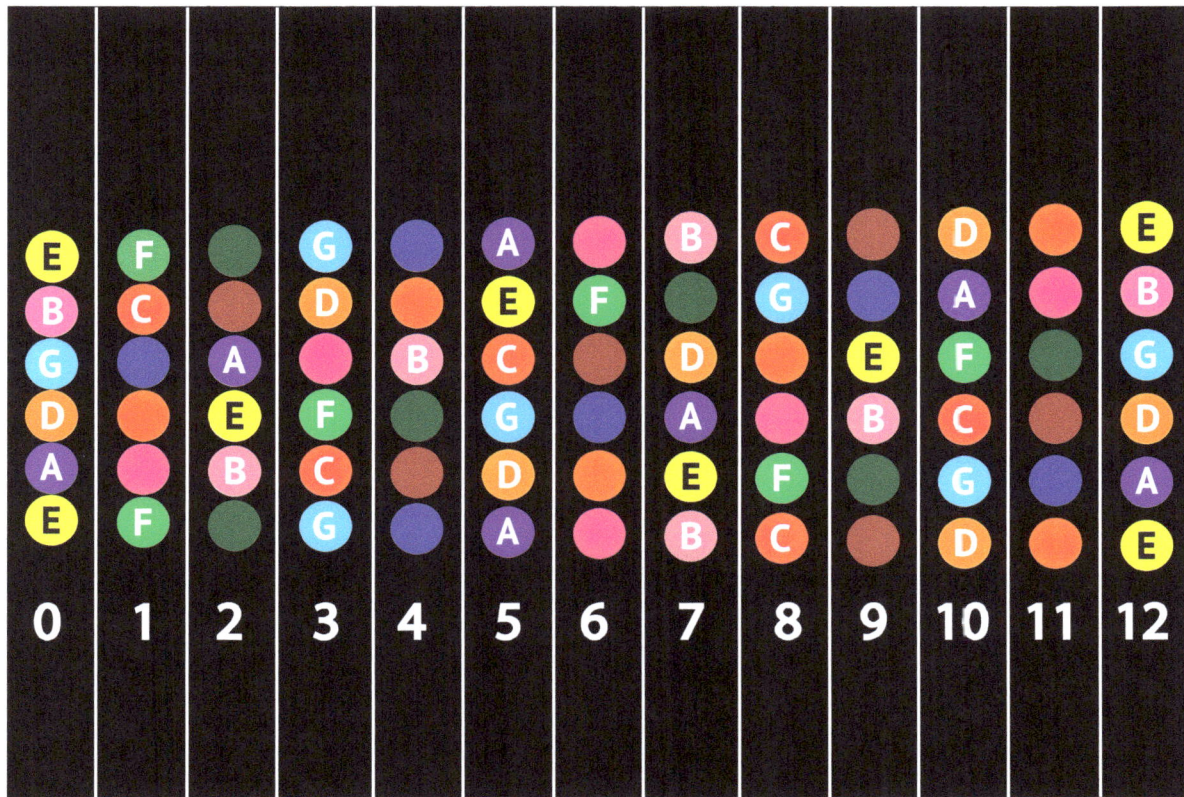

Full Size Wide-Neck Acoustic Guitar (Age 12+)

Congratulations!

(your name here)

worked hard
and completed

Play It!
LEVEL 1

Christmas Songs
for Guitar

Make sure your

Play It!

library is complete

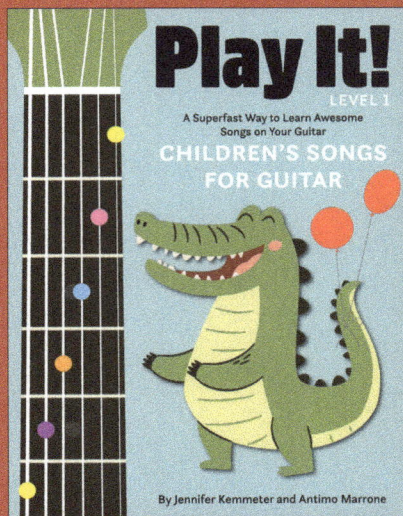

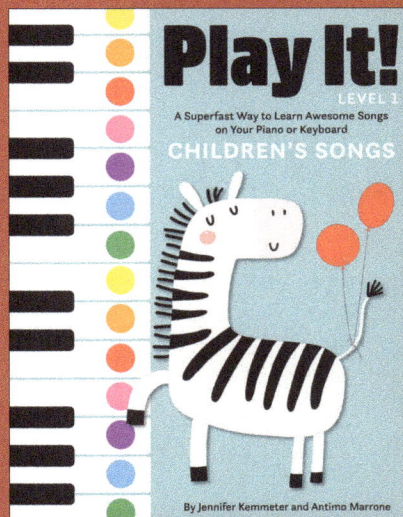

www.ingramcontent.com/pod-product-compliance
Lightning Source LLC
Chambersburg PA
CBHW060859090426

42737CB00026B/3497